First Lady Manual

First Lady Manual

A practical guide for Christian wives

DEBORAH GIBSON HOLLOWAY

Charleston, SC
www.PalmettoPublishing.com

First Lady Manual:
A practical guide for Christian wives

Published by Deborah Gibson Holloway
Copyright © 2021 by Deborah Gibson Holloway

Bible quotations are from:
The Holy Bible, The King James Version (KJV) or the New King James Version (NKJV) unless otherwise stated.

For information:
Deborah Gibson Holloway
Cup Family International Ministries
Durham, North Carolina

Hardcover ISBN: 978-1-68515-255-0
Paperback ISBN: 978-1-68515-256-7
eBook ISBN: 978-1-68515-257-4

Dedication

This book is dedicated to my mother Sarah Gibson Green, my maternal grandmother Nettie, paternal grandmother Della, and my mothers-in-love J.Linn, Ollie Jane and Elder Mother Patricia Graham. These are and were the First Ladies in my life, and without them I would not be who I am today. I am thankful for the wisdom, love and instruction I have received from them throughout my years.

To my dads William and Albert, and my children Derrick, Terrence, Linda, Paul and Linwood. I'm thankful for you being in my life. I love you and pray God's continued grace, peace and blessings upon you.

To my husband, Apostle Johnny Holloway, God ordained, full of strength and wisdom, who truly loves God and me.

Table of Contents

Thankfulness

I am thankful to all who made a contribution to this book in any way.

First of all, I thank my LORD and Savior Jesus Christ for showing me the great need for this manual and putting it on my heart to write it.

I thank my husband, Apostle Dr. Johnny Holloway, founder of Cup of Salvation Deliverance Church and Ministries, Inc. at Durham, N.C. and Cup Family International Ministries. He is my husband of 47 years alongside whom I served in ministry for twenty three years in senior leadership. I thank him for supporting me in this effort and I thank him for his abounding continual love.

I am thankful to my children for their encouragement and support. I offer special thanks to Terrence, Derrick and Linwood for being my *"Johnny on the spot"* when I had a need.

Also a special thank you to First Lady Pastor Sharon Marshall for being a true friend and Sister in Christ Jesus.

And I am thankful for you... May you always remember that you are the daughter of The Most High King and He has great plans for your life.

I say to you now, "Arise and go forth. It is in you to accomplish great things on this earth for Christ Jesus. Be About It!"

Introduction

When the Lord called me into ministry as a "First Lady", I did not receive any instructions or have a full understanding of what was required of me as the wife of a Senior Pastor. I did have a basic understanding that ministry is a sacrifice, and I knew that I had to submit myself to the will of God and not stand in His way as He used my husband and me for His called work. However, I had no real understanding of all that the ministry actually entailed.

Therefore ladies, if you know within yourself that you are not in a place of submission and support of your husband in this area, be very truthful and let him know your concerns. The position of the Pastor's wife intertwines your life into the lives of vulnerable people and the Lord will not hold you guiltless if you step in willingly and fail to do His work. Your walk will not be just about you, your feelings and your agenda; rather your walk is to be a set apart work called of God. This ministry is for the greater good of the Kingdom of Christ, and there is a lot of good you can do through the ministry of "First Lady" if you will allow Christ and His Holy Spirit to lead.

I pray God's continued blessings upon you as you follow Him.

This book is for every Pastor's wife, and for every woman who desires to be a wife. You may not be a "First Lady" in a ministry at this time, but as a wife and/or a pastor's wife, the information contained herein is very relevant to your Christian walk.

I pray that every woman who reads this book will gain knowledge, and that God will give you the wisdom and understanding to rightly apply your knowledge. As God opens your eyes, I pray that you will open your heart to receive what you need to assist you in your walk as a First Lady.

1 Peter 3:12 For the eyes of the Lord are over the righteous, and his ears are open unto their prayers: but the face of the Lord is against them that do evil.

Unless otherwise stated, all Bible passages are from the King James Version (KJV) or the New King James Version (NKJV).

How this book came about:

Through the years I often heard "You don't act like most First Ladies" and I would usually reply, "I didn't get the book." Thus, this manual...

This manual is a practical guide written to help you serve God and His ordained man at the very best and highest level of consistent ethical standards.

Who is a "First Lady"?

*T*he title, " First Lady" is usually defined as the female spouse of selected heads of state and of Senior male Pastors. When this title was first used for the President's wife, it referred to her as the first lady in the land because her husband was the official head of the nation. In the church, the Senior Pastor's wife is often given this title of respect.

The Senior Pastor is the leader of the church and the First Lady is also a leader in the church. A leader is one who influences others to follow a specific plan, or one who organizes a group of people to achieve a common goal. One of your specific duties will be to instill in the congregants a desire to follow the stated vision of the ministry.

And the Lord God said, It is not good that the man should be alone; I will make him an help-meet for him. Genesis 2:18
This is a faithful saying: If a man desires the position of a bishop, he desires a good work. 1 Timothy 3:1

Likewise, their wives must be reverent, not slanderers, temperate, faithful in all things. 1 Timothy 3:11 But we have this treasure in earthen vessels, that the excellency of the power may be of God, and not of us. 1 Cor 4:7-12

To serve well in the role of "First Lady", you have to see it for what it really is. It is a call for you to stand with the man of God as he submits himself in service to the LORD. You are called to help him meet his obligations to God and to God's people. In order to get the walk right, you must immerse yourself in Christ and chase hard after Him at all times. Your relationship with the people in the ministry is important, but your relationship with the Lord Jesus Christ is paramount. Develop your intimate relationship with him by prayer and worship, by reading and studying His Word, and fasting. In this way, you will continue to develop into a mature Christian and a treasured ministry leader.

As followers of Christ, our walk should look different from that of the world. A Christian should lead others in the right way according to God's Word, being doers of the Word and not hearers only (James1:22). Right standing with God, and personal and public integrity are absolutely essential in your position.

Walk in Integrity

Spiritual Maturity

This word *integrity* is derived from the Latin word *integer* which means complete or whole.

Hebrews 10:22-25 says "Let us draw near with a true heart in full assurance of faith, having our hearts sprinkled from an evil conscience, and our bodies washed with pure water. Let us hold fast the profession of our faith without wavering; (for he is faithful that promised;)"

You must be complete and confident within yourself; it is essential that you know who you are, nothing wavering, or you may begin to harbor feelings of doubt, fear, and unbelief.

You may feel as though some people are against you, but you have to believe that God has prepared you for your husband and your husband for you.

Know that He is preparing you daily for the role of Pastor's wife or "First Lady"; therefore, do not walk in doubt. Walk in faith, nothing wavering.

Sometimes I too was unsure. I had never walked this path before, but with God in me and the encouraging faith of my family and other Christians, I was able to do this work. My strength was renewed. I believed that the Spirit of Christ that lives in me would make me able to accomplish being a proper First Lady and He did.

I say to you today, stay close to Christ Jesus. Have faith in Him and develop your courting relationship with Him daily. Believe in yourself. Move forward and do not doubt God nor you.

Walk in Wholeness,
Forgiveness is the key to healing

*I*t is imperative, from the very start of ministry, that you know yourself. Know who you are and do not walk in shame, for it is not from God. The Bible says, "**For all have sinned and come short of the glory of God**", and "**there is none righteous, no not one**", other than by and through the Blood of Jesus Christ our Savior.

When I became saved "for real", I asked God and others whom I had wronged to forgive me, and I started to walk and live according to God's word. In the process of the change taking place in my life, I lost friends, and people who did not want Christ (for real) separated from me. That's not all bad because your walk must always continue towards Christ; you can not allow others to pull you back into worldliness.

By forgiving others, you are freeing yourself from hurt, bondage and shame and walking into complete freedom. Yes, claim your freedom, because failing to forgive is bondage. It is a trap that the enemy uses against us. As I moved forward in forgiveness, I learned to forgive myself as well as others, after which I was able to walk in the love, mercy, grace, peace and the promises of God. There is no need for you to have anxiety or be in distress about your role because God has called you to it and He is well able to equip you in the position. You are a winner and winners know who they are. Walk forward into the calling and accomplish at your highest level. Remember, you are not alone; God the Father is with you.

Know Who You Are

I once heard Christian leader Mike Murdock say that our "Self-portrait decides our self-confidence and conduct" and I have found it to be true. In other words, your thought portrait of who you are determines your confidence and your conduct. The way you see yourself becomes who you are! Some of us think too highly of ourselves, and some don't think highly enough. You are not perfect, so you dare not put yourself on a pedestal; however, all of your disgrace and shame were eradicated when you asked Jesus to take it away. Hold your head up and become who God has predestined you to be. Believe in God and believe in yourself.

Resist the enemy's plan to cause you to think that other women have an ungodly interest in your husband, or that other women are better than you, because that is not true. Some women may indeed be envious of you and the relationship you have with your husband, but you've got to remember that he is YOUR husband and you already have him. Do not allow the enemy to diminish your confidence in who you are. Your husband chose you because it is you that he loves and wants. Walk in assurance of who you are in every area of your life, including your marital status, with your head held high, even during times you may not feel like it. He is yours; treat him well and you will always have him. God has already officially selected and ordained you his wife.

Walk in righteousness and habitually choose Christ in everything. Although the world places strong pressure upon us as Christians to follow its path, we must make the decision daily to follow Christ and lead others to do so as well. Be a person with a strong moral stance, a person of your word. Let the character of Christ be evident and shine through in your life. You are a daughter of The King. Be aware at all times that many others will be watching your life and imitating you.

As the First Lady, what you have to give to the congregation is the genuine love of Christ. Don't be the type of First Lady who is standoffish. Know that "church hurt" is real (it may have even happened to you at some point). People come from all walks of life into a church building. We have to remember that we are the true church when we have the heart and mind of Christ. As kids, some of my friends and I would interlace our fingers together and say, "this is the church and this is the steeple, open the door and you'll see the people". Some of the people who come have tremendous hurt, and what they will need from you is tremendous genuine love. Your genuine love will comfort and help to heal a multitude of pain.

Bring the Outcome

*B*ecause you are the First Lady, many will desire to have a positive relationship with you. This is a plus. Don't cause damage. The way that each of your encounters with others turns out will be totally up to you. What will be your response to the encounter? What is your desired end result for it? You bring the outcome.

You will meet challenges. The phrase "demon deacons" doesn't just apply to the Wake Forest basketball team. That phrase probably was coined a long time before the team ever appeared on the scene. It may have stemmed from encounters and actions taken by church men in leadership who did not read their Bibles and/or display the character of Jesus Christ. You may meet some of these men (and women) in your walk as a First Lady. Refuse to let them sway you towards the negative. Remember who you are at all times!

Your Marriage, Your First Ministry

Love That Man

God is always looking at our marriages; He has his eyes on what occurs in our homes because nothing is more important than your marriage in God's eyes. Your marriage IS your ministry. Let each person line up behind their head.

But I would have you know, that the head of every man is Christ; and the head of the woman is the man; and the head of Christ is God. 1 Corinthians 11:3 For the husband is the head of the wife, even as Christ is the head of the church: and he is the saviour of the body. Ephesians 5:23

Cover Him in Love and Prayer

The heart of her husband doth safely trust in her...She will do him good and not evil all the days of her life. Proverbs 31:11a,12

Husband and wife are God ordained positions in Holy Matrimony. You've made a vow to one another, and to God.

To have a successful marriage, a husband and wife MUST pray. They should pray and spend time with God on a daily basis. They should pray with each other as well as individually. Every individual has to develop his/her own relationship with Christ. Spouses should always pray for each other.

Prov 23:7 As he thinks in his heart, so is he.

Love that Man!

*P*ut the focus on him, he is Your personal ministry. After God, he is your first ministry. Anticipate his needs and even some of his desires. Never cause him to question whether or not you love him, or whether you are for him and with him. Show him that you love him everyday and in every way. There is a great book for married couples written by Gary Chapman, titled "The Five Love Languages". One of the languages is Acts of Service. I have learned that my husband enjoys that language as well as Quality Time.

A couple of things my husband likes is to have his feet and legs lotioned, and for the bed to be turned back in the evenings. Because I already know that this is something he likes, when he comes home in the evenings I have the lotion sitting out where he can see it and I have the bed turned back. Simple things, but meaningful to him.

Why do I do this? It is because I want him to know that he is the most adored person in my life.

"Happy spouse, happy house", Yes! Both of you need peace and happiness. Let your husband know how special he is to you and he will reciprocate your love. Special affection and attention will be returned to you. Your marriage and your ministry will flourish.

You'll be secure in the knowledge that no one can capture his heart because it belongs to you. Find your husband's language and speak it to him clearly and consistently (and also tell him yours).

"The heart of her husband doth safely trust in her, so that he shall have no need of spoil."
Proverbs 31:11

Our Children, Our Heritage

Legacy

Behold, children are a heritage from the LORD,
The fruit of the womb is a reward.
Like arrows in the hand of a warrior,
So are the children of one's youth.
Happy is the man who has his quiver full of them;
Psalm 127:3–5

Your wife shall be like a fruitful vine
In the very heart of your house,
Your children like olive plants
All around your table.
Psalm 128:3

Train up a child in the way he should go,
And when he is old he will not depart from it.
Proverbs 22:6

Have you ever observed a child's behavior while you were in a restaurant, airport or school setting or even at church?

The behaviors they display are learned from their home environment.

Children become who we adults train them to be. We should train them up in the love and nurture of the LORD.

Therefore parents, as the Bible says, it is our responsibility to train up the child and not to allow them to just grow up. Don't allow your child to flounder in despair and confusion of not knowing who they are to be because you as their parent have not given them guidance and direction. This is your legacy. Teach them to pray and read God's word daily so they will have something to stand on in the good times and during the bad. Lead and train them well.

In the USA and some other countries, one is considered a child from birth to the age of seventeen years. They are in a constant state of learning during this time.

Their brains are developing and taking in information whether it's positive or negative. We as parents are like the project managers of their lives, and should give them focused guidance and attention.

When you are focused on something (or someone), you are paying special attention to it therefore it becomes a main focal point.

Ladies as the mother and "First Lady" in your child's life, you are to counsel them in wisdom, encourage them in faith, and direct them in love. Give them a stable foundation to grow on and they will always come back to seek guidance and wisdom nuggets.

There is a great book that you will want, written by Dr. Johnny Holloway, titled "Train Up A Child" which gives timeless strategies for guiding a child from youth into mature adulthood.

Suggested Codes of Conduct

*C*odes of Conduct are instructions put in place to help an individual succeed in a particular community. Growing up in your childhood home, perhaps your parents had rules to make it clear that there were certain ways to act at your house. Most of us quickly realized that if we were going to be successful there or be a part of the family, we needed to follow the program. As adults, we make our own rules in our own houses. It is like that in every strata of society; there are certain rules and laws that govern us, so as to preclude everyone doing what is right in their own minds.

Etiquette - The customary code of respectful and considerate (polite) behavior in society or of a community of people.

But as he which hath called you is holy, so be ye holy in all manner of conversation (conduct or communication)... 1 Peter 1:15

Speech - **A soft answer turneth away wrath: but grievous words stir up anger.**
The tongue of the wise useth knowledge aright: but the mouth of fools poureth out foolishness.
Proverbs 15:1,2

Is there more to be said? The word of God gives us the knowledge and wisdom we need to help ourselves and our spouses prosper God's people. When we move away from selfish ambition and motivation, ministry work as the First Lady can and will be joyous and rewarding.

She openeth her mouth with wisdom; and in her tongue is the law of kindness.
Proverbs 31:26

When we speak with kindness and offer words of wisdom to the congregation, the ministry will be better for it. You are to exhort the congregation. Speak words of encouragement and hope into their lives. They will find hope in the ministry, and in the positive energy that the Pastor and the First Lady bring to it. Your caring and kind support is vital to the life of the ministry.

Dress

*A*nd take thou unto thee Aaron thy brother, and his sons with him, from among the children of Israel, that he may minister unto me in the priest's office,...

And thou shalt make holy garments for Aaron thy brother for glory and for beauty. Exodus 28:1,2

Who can find a virtuous woman? for her price is far above rubies.
The heart of her husband doth safely trust in her, so that he shall have no need of spoil. She will do him good and not evil all the days of her life. She girdeth her loins with strength, and strengtheneth her arms.
She maketh herself coverings of tapestry; her clothing is silk and purple.
Proverbs 31:10,11,17,22

Each denomination is different regarding the matter of dress, so depending on whether you are Methodist, Baptist, Catholic, Jewish, Pentecostal, or non-Denominational, I recommend that you confer with the leaders in your church affiliation for best results. What holds true for every denomination that I've encountered is cleanliness and neatness in appearance. Your physical appearance matters. The manner in which you present yourself speaks to others, and first impressions are particularly important. You always want to look and feel pretty, but you also want to be comfortable, because some church functions can last several hours.

As you minister in the office of First Lady, the glory of the Lord is upon you and He has given you His beauty for your ashes.

Visiting Churches

When an outside church is visiting your home church, do your very best to make the visiting First Lady feel welcome. Greet her when she arrives and have a seat prepared for her beside yours. An extra lap cloth, mints and water for her may be appropriate also. If the visiting First Lady chooses to sit with her husband or congregation, that is perfectly fine. When you are going to a church that you have not visited before, usually you won't go wrong when you wear a dress or skirt, hose and heels. Hose may not be necessary, but they do make your legs look pretty and can make a shoe feel more comfortable. Wearing a flat or low heeled dress shoe is also appropriate.

Fashion and Style

*I*n modest apparel that professes godliness...

Why would a married woman show cleavage? I personally don't think it is right for women to be held responsible for the whims and thoughts of men, because all mankind will be held accountable by God for their own actions, thoughts and deeds. However, the real issue is doing what pleases the Lord.

Yes, we like to look nice and it is nice to be fashionable to some degree in church, but remember it is the house of God and not the club or a runway. Keep your dress appropriate for the Lord's house, always being mindful that others look to you to set the example

If you are wearing a dress or skirt, knee length is modest apparel, because you know what happens to the hemline when you sit down. I suggest that you carry your own lap cloth with you when visiting other churches, or you may be offered the giant throw used to cover people who kneel at the altar (this has happened to me before; accept this word of wisdom). If you are offered a lap cloth or throw and don't have your own, receive the offered one with cheerfulness, for you are being told, nicely, that you need one.

The Hat

*A*h, the First Lady hat. We have been wearing that First Lady hat for decades. It is a thing of beauty. It makes us look sophisticated. It makes me feel two feet taller.

It is a fashion statement. You can hide under it. You love it. You hate it. Is it required?

How and when do You wear it? So many thoughts, comments and questions...

In most churches today, it is not a necessity; it is simply a preference. If you enjoy wearing a hat, continue doing so, just don't have it so high and/ or wide that the person sitting beside or behind you regrets that you wore it because it is obstructing their line of vision. Be mindful of others at all times. It may be necessary to have several nice wigs, because "bad hair" days happen. It is better to present yourself in a nice wig rather than with unkempt hair.

Refresh and Replenish

Self Care

Exodus 23:12
Six days thou shalt do thy work, and on the seventh day thou shalt rest: that thine ox and thine ass may rest, and the son of thy handmaid, and the stranger, may be refreshed.

Mark 6:31
And he said unto them, Come ye yourselves apart into a desert place, and rest a while: for there were many coming and going, and they had no leisure so much as to eat.

Ladies it is vitally important that you take good care of yourself. In the process of working a job, taking care of your husband, your children, congregational members and others, it is so important that you get your proper rest and relaxation.

I take a day for myself weekly to refresh and replenish, to do nothing or to do what I want to do that is relaxing for me. Aside from studying the word of God, I love listening to music, reading novels, mani-pedis, facials, leisurely walking and window shopping.

Find what replenishes you and make sure you schedule a day weekly to enjoy it.

Conclusion

*I*n the coming years, how will the people of God remember you?

Will it be as a woman who stood with the man of God as he cared for God's people or as one who ran off and hid so as not to be bothered? Will you be remembered as one who brought disdain and discord to God's house? It is totally up to you. I have a great hope and prayer that this manual will give you some insight and understanding of your Christian calling. I exhort you to "Arise and Walk forward" in the strength, grace and favor that God has granted you.

Your availability as First Lady will be strength and hope to the congregants of the church in which God has placed you. It will help that ministry obtain the peace and comfort it needs. Comfort brings calmness. If the congregants see that their Pastor and First Lady are at peace with each other, the love in the Ministry is expanded all the more. Go forth and do the work that God is calling you to do, and always give it your very best effort.

Being confident of this very thing, that he which hath begun a good work in you will perform it until the day of Jesus Christ: Philippians 1:6

Prayer

May The Lord bless thee, and keep thee:

May The Lord make his face shine upon thee, and

be gracious unto thee:

May The Lord our God lift up his countenance

upon thee, and give thee peace.

In Jesus name. Amen

Self-Examination

As the First Lady, where do I see myself in this ministry?

_____

_____

Am I looking through my eyes or seeing with God's sight?

_____

_____

What do I have to offer the congregation?

_____

_____

What do they have to offer me?

_____

_____

What is the cost?

_____

_____

Am I willing to pay the price?

_____

_____

Will I be a help to the Senior Pastor or will I be a hindrance?

_____

_____

How will I be his helpmeet? Lord, show me.

_____

_____

Will my interaction in the ministry be Godly?

_____

_____

Am I being considerate of the needs of others and showing kindness?

_____

_____

What Fruit of God's Spirit am I exhibiting (Galatians 5:22, 23)?

_____

_____

AFFIRMATIONS

I CAN DO ALL THINGS THROUGH CHRIST,
for HE is my STRENGTH!

I WILL ALWAYS PRAY AND SEEK CHRIST
FOR GUIDANCE.

LORD, IF YOU CAN USE ME,
I AM WILLING AND AVAILABLE.

CPSIA information can be obtained
at www.ICGtesting.com
Printed in the USA
BVHW060824281221
625045BV00018B/623